CHRISTMAS SHEET MUSIC HITS

Product Line Manager: Carol Cuellar
Project Manager: Zobeida Pérez
Cover Design: Joe Klucar

CONTENTS

FROSTY THE SNOWMAN

Words and Music by
STEVE NELSON and JACK ROLLINS

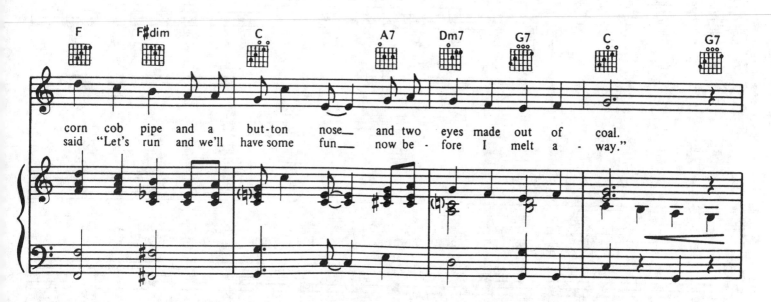

Frosty the Snowman - 3 - 1

ANGELS WE HAVE HEARD ON HIGH

TRADITIONAL

Angels We Have Heard on High - 2 - 1

CHRISTMAS AULD LANG SYNE

Words and Music by
MANN CURTIS and FRANK MILITARY

CHRISTMAS MEM'RIES

Words by
ALAN and MARILYN BERGMAN

Music by
DON COSTA

Christmas Mem'ries - 3 - 1

11

Christmas Mem'ries - 3 - 2

THE CHRISTMAS WALTZ

Words by
SAMMY CAHN

Music by
JULE STYNE

The Christmas Waltz - 3 - 1

14

DON'T SAVE IT ALL FOR CHRISTMAS DAY

Words and Music by
PETER ZIZZO, RIC WAKE
and CELINE DION

Don't Save It All for Christmas Day - 7 - 1

19

Don't Save It All for Christmas Day - 7 - 4

Verse 2:
How could you wait another minute,
A hug is warmer when you're in it.
And, baby, that's a fact.
And sayin' I love you's always better,
Seasons, reasons, they don't matter.
So don't hold back.
How many people in this world
So needful in this world?
How many people are praying for love?
(To Chorus:)

THE FIRST NOEL

TRADITIONAL

THE GIFT

Words and Music by
JIM BRICKMAN and
TOM DOUGLAS

Slowly ♩ = 72

(with pedal)

Verse 1:

1. Win-ter snow is fall-ing__ down, chil-dren laugh-ing all a-round.

Lights are turn-ing on, like a fair-y tale__ come true.__ Sit-tin' by the fire we__ made.

The Gift - 5 - 1

GRANDMA GOT RUN OVER
BY A REINDEER

Words and Music by
RANDY BROOKS

Grand-ma got run o-ver by a rein-deer

walk-ing home from our house Christ-mas Eve.

You can say there's no such thing as San-ta, but

Grandma Got Run Over by a Reindeer - 5 - 1

Verse 2:
Now we're all so proud of Grandpa,
He's been taking this so well.
See him in there watching football,
Drinking beer and playing cards with Cousin Mel.
It's not Christmas without Grandma.
All the family's dressed in black,
And we just can't help but wonder:
Should we open up her gifts or send them back?

(To Chorus:)

Verse 3:
Now the goose is on the table,
And the pudding made of fig,
And the blue and silver candles,
That would just have matched the hair in Grandma's wig.
I've warned all my friends and neighbors,
Better watch out for yourselves.
They should never give a license
To a man who drives a sleigh and plays with elves.

(To Chorus:)

GROWN-UP CHRISTMAS LIST

Words and Music by
DAVID FOSTER and
LINDA THOMPSON JENNER

Grown-up Christmas List - 5 - 1

HARK! THE HERALD ANGELS SING

Words by
CHARLES WESLEY

Music by
FELIX MENDELSSOHN

Hark! the Herald Angels Sing - 3 - 1

40

Hark! the Herald Angels Sing - 3 - 2

HAVE YOURSELF A MERRY
LITTLE CHRISTMAS

Words and Music by
HUGH MARTIN and RALPH BLANE

I DON'T WANT TO BE ALONE
FOR CHRISTMAS
(Unless I'm Alone With You)

Words and Music by
DIANE WARREN

I'LL BE HOME FOR CHRISTMAS

Lyric by
KIM GANNON

Music by
WALTER KENT

I'll Be Home for Christmas - 2 - 1

IT CAME UPON THE MIDNIGHT CLEAR

Words by
EDMUND H. SEARS

Music by
RICHARD S. WILLIS

will   to   men,   from   Heav - en's   all   gra -   cious
low -   ly   plains   they   bend ___   on   hov - er - ing

King." ___   The   world   in   sol - emn   still - ness
wing. ___   And   ev - er   o - ver   its   Ba - bel

lay   to   hear   the   an - gels   sing. ___
sounds   the   bless - ed   an - gels   sing. ___

3.   And ye beneath life's crushing load,
      Whose forms are bending low,
      Who toil along the climbing way
      With painful steps and slow,
      Look now! for glad and golden hours
      Come swiftly on the wing.
      O rest beside the weary road
      And hear the angels sing.

4.   For lo, the days are hast'ning on,
      By prophet bards foretold,
      When with the ever circling years
      Comes round the age of gold,
      When peace shall over all the earth
      Its ancient splendor fling,
      And the whole world give back the song
      Which now the angels sing.

IT WOULDN'T BE CHRISTMAS WITHOUT YOU

By SCOTT KRIPPAYNE
and JOHN TESH

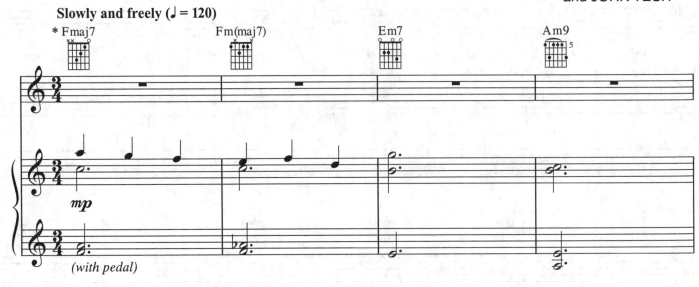

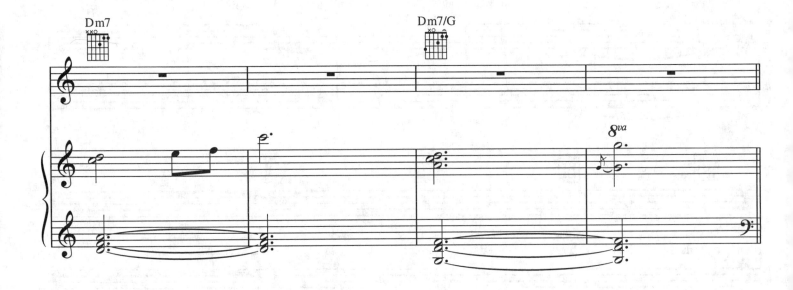

*Original recording in key of D♭.

It Wouldn't Be Christmas Without You - 4 - 1

IT'S THE MOST WONDERFUL
TIME OF THE YEAR

By
EDDIE POLA and GEORGE WYLE

It's the Most Wonderful Time of the Year - 3 - 1

It's the Most Wonderful Time of the Year - 3 - 2

JINGLE-BELL ROCK

Words and Music by
JOE BEAL and JIM BOOTHE

Moderately (with a rock beat)

Chorus

Jin - gle - bell, Jin - gle - bell, JIN - GLE - BELL ROCK__ Jin - gle - bell swing and

Jin - gle - bells ring Snow - in' and blow - in' up bush - els of fun

Jingle-Bell Rock - 3 - 1

JOY TO THE WORLD

Words by
ISAAC WATTS

Music by
GEORGE F. HANDEL

Joy to the World - 2 - 2

LET IT SNOW! LET IT SNOW! LET IT SNOW!

Words by
SAMMY CAHN

Music by
JULE STYNE

Moderato

(Rhythmic but not too fast)

Oh! the weath-er out-side is fright-ful But the fire is so de-light-ful And

since we've no place to go, LET IT SNOW! LET IT SNOW! LET IT SNOW! It

does-n't show signs of stop-ping And I brought some corn for pop-ping; The

Let It Snow! Let It Snow! Let It Snow! - 2 - 1

THE LITTLE DRUMMER BOY

Words and Music by
KATHERINE DAVIS, HENRY ONORATI
and HARRY SIMEONE

The Little Drummer Boy - 4 - 1

The Little Drummer Boy - 4 - 2

The Little Drummer Boy - 4 - 4

NUTTIN' FOR CHRISTMAS

Words and Music by
SID TEPPER and ROY C. BENNETT

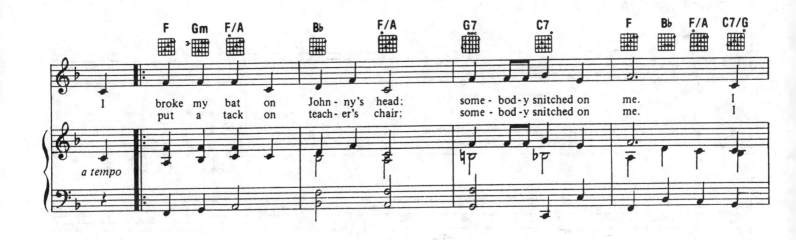

I broke my bat on John-ny's head; some-bod-y snitched on me. I
put a tack on teach-er's chair; some-bod-y snitched on me. I

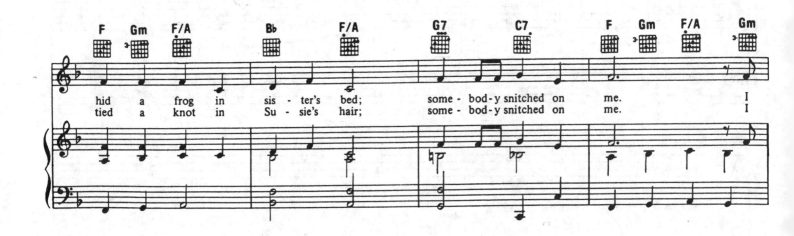

hid a frog in sis-ter's bed; some-bod-y snitched on me. I
tied a knot in Su-sie's hair; some-bod-y snitched on me. I

Nuttin' for Christmas - 3 - 1

3. I won't be seeing Santa Claus; somebody snitched on me.
He won't come visit me because somebody snitched on me.
Next year I'll be going straight, next year I'll be good, just wait,
I'd start now but it's too late; somebody snitched on me. Oh,

SANTA BABY

Words and Music by
JOAN JAVITS, PHILIP SPRINGER
and TONY SPRINGER

Mis-ter "Claus," I feel as tho I know ya ____ So you won't mind if I should get fam-

mil-ya, will ya? San-ta Ba-by, just slip a sa-ble un-der the tree ____
San-ta Ba-by, one lit-tle thing I real-ly do need;

____ for me. ____ Been an aw-ful good girl ____ San-ta Ba-by, So
____ The deed ____ to a pla-tin-um mine San-ta hon-ey, So

Santa Baby - 3 - 1

hur – ry down the chim – ney to - night.

hur – ry down the chim – ney to - night.

San ta Ba –by, a fif – ty four con – vert – i –ble, too, light blue.

San ta cu –tie and fill my stock – ing with a du – plex and cheques.

I'll wait up for you dear Santa Ba – by, so hur – ry down the chim – ney to - night.

Sign your X on the line Santa cu – tie and hur – ry down the chim – ney to - night.

Think of all the fun I've missed.

Come and trim my Christ- mas tree

O HOLY NIGHT
(Cantique de Noel)

By
ADOLPHE CHARLES ADAM

O Holy Night - 2 - 1

SANTA CLAUS IS COMIN' TO TOWN

Words by
HAVEN GILLESPIE

Music by
J. FRED COOTS

Santa Claus Is Comin' to Town - 2 - 1

WE WISH YOU A MERRY CHRISTMAS

TRADITIONAL ENGLISH FOLK SONG

We Wish You a Merry Christmas - 2 - 1

WINTER WONDERLAND

Words by
DICK SMITH

Music by
FELIX BERNARD

Winter Wonderland - 2 - 1

SILENT NIGHT

Words and Music by
JOSEPH MOHR and
FRANZ GRUBER

Si - lent Night, Ho - ly Night, All is calm, all is bright, round yon vir - gin Moth - er and child. Ho - ly in - fant so ten - der and mild. Sleep in heav - en - ly

Silent Night - 3 - 1

88

SLEIGH RIDE

Words by
MITCHELL PARISH

Music by
LEROY ANDERSON

Moderately bright

Just hear those sleigh bells jin - gle - ing, ring - ting - tin - gle - ing, too, __

__ Come on, it's love - ly weath - er for a Sleigh Ride to - geth - er with you, __

__ Out - side the snow is fall - ing and friends are call - ing "Yoo hoo," __

Sleigh Ride - 3 - 1

THE TWELVE DAYS OF CHRISTMAS

TRADITIONAL ENGLISH

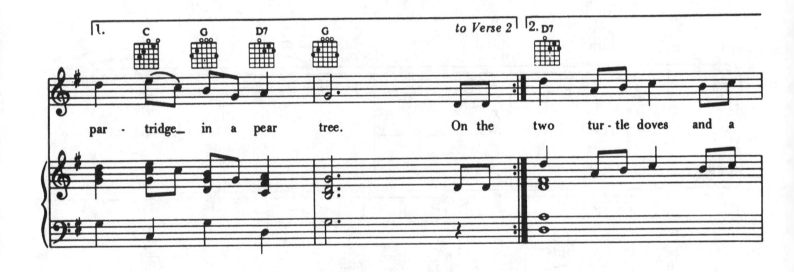

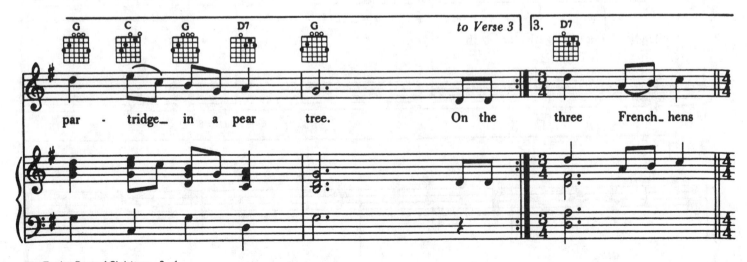

The Twelve Days of Christmas - 3 - 1

94

WHAT CHILD IS THIS?
(GREENSLEEVES)

By WILLIAM C. DIX
Based on GREENSLEEVES,
an Old English Air

SENDING YOU A LITTLE CHRISTMAS

Words and Music by
JIM BRICKMAN, VICTORIA SHAW
and BILLY MANN

Moderately, with swing feel ♩ = 102

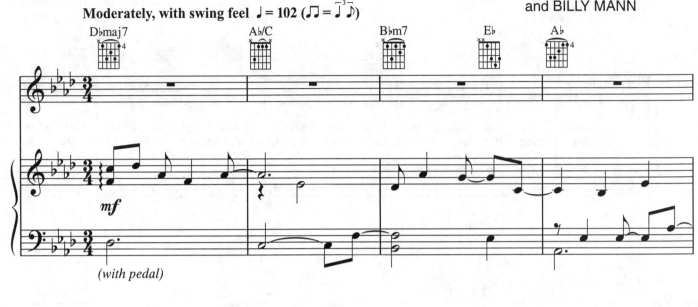

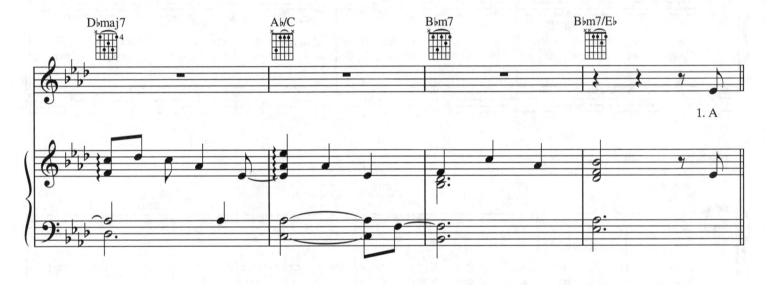

Verse:

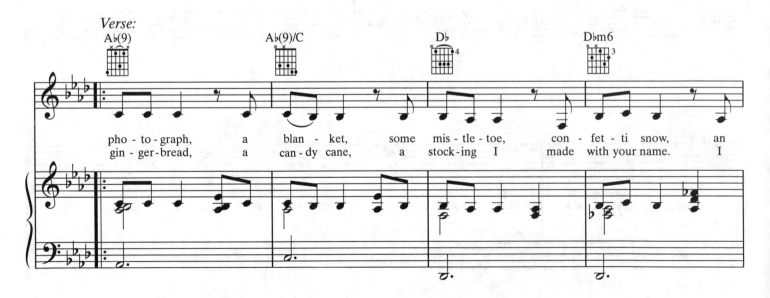

pho - to - graph, a blan - ket, some mis - tle - toe, con - fet - ti snow, an

gin - ger - bread, a can - dy cane, a stock - ing I made with your name. I

an - gel to put on a tree._____
filled it with your fa - v'rite things._____

a

San - ta Claus in cray - on, to make you smile__ to - day,
way to say "I love you," like kiss - es through__ the air,

while you're so far a - way._____
hop - ing you feel me there._____

𝄋 *Chorus:*

So I'm send - ing you a lit - tle Christ - mas,